ROLES 'N MINISTRY

Bunch

12 studies for
individuals or groups

CREATED MALE & FEMALE BIBLE STUDIES

*With Study Notes & Guidelines
for Leaders*

INTERVARSITY PRESS
DOWNERS GROVE, ILLINOIS 60515

MW01519431

To the ministers of Fifth Avenue Baptist Church,
Huntington, West Virginia, with thanks
for their encouragement:
Dr. R. F. Smith, Rev. Michael Williams
and Rev. Frederick Lewis.

® 1993 by Cindy Bunch

InterVarsity Press® is the book-publishing division of InterVarsity Christian Fellowship®, a student movement active on campus at hundreds of universities, colleges and schools of nursing in the United States of America, and a member movement of the International Fellowship of Evangelical Students. For information about local and regional activities, write Public Relations Dept., InterVarsity Christian Fellowship, 6400 Schroeder Rd., P.O. Box 7895, Madison, WI 53707-7895.

All Scripture quotations, unless otherwise indicated, are from the HOLY BIBLE, NEW INTERNATIONAL VERSION®. NIV®· Copyright ©1973, 1978, 1984 by International Bible Society. Used by permission of Zondervan Publishing House. All rights reserved.

Cartoon on p. 31 taken from Church Is Stranger Than Fiction ©1990 by Mary Chambers and used by permission of InterVarsity Press.

Cover photograph: Michael Goss

ISBN 0-8308-1134-6

Printed in the United States of America ∞

15	14	13	12	11	10	9	8	7	6	5	4	3	2	1

04	03	02	01	00	99	98	97	96	95	94	93

Getting the Most out of Created Male & Female Bible Studies

Created Male and Female Bible Studies are designed to help us understand what it means to be created in the image of God. We know that God had a purpose in creating two sexes. Discovering gender distinctions is an exciting and intriguing part of what it means to be human. But sometimes it is confusing and frustrating as well. These studies will help us understand what God's purpose is for us individually and as a part of the human race.

The passages you will study will be challenging, inspiring and practical. They will show you how to think about your sexuality and how you live that out. And they will help you to better understand what the other sex is about—breaking down stereotypes and helping you find new ways to communicate.

These guides are not designed merely to convince you of the truthfulness of some idea held by the authors. Rather, they are intended to guide you into discovering biblical truths that will renew your heart and mind. How? Through an inductive approach to Bible study. Rather than simply telling you what they believe, the authors will lead you to discover what the Bible says about a particular topic through a series of questions. These studies will help you to think about the meaning of the passage so that you can truly understand what the biblical writer intended to say. Additionally, these studies are personal. At the end of each study, you'll be given an opportunity to make a commitment to respond—to take steps toward changing the way you think and act. And you'll find guidance for prayer as well. Finally, these studies are versatile. They are designed for student, professional, neighborhood and/or church groups. They are also effective for individual study.

How They're Put Together
Created Male and Female Bible Studies have a distinctive workbook format with space for writing a response to each question. This format is ideal for personal study and allows group members to prepare in advance for the discussion or write down notes during the study. Each study takes about forty-five minutes in a group setting or thirty minutes in personal study—unless you choose to take more time.

At the end of the guide are some study notes. They do not give "the answers," but they do provide additional background information on certain questions to help you through the difficult spots. In addition, the "Guidelines for Leaders" section describes how to lead a group discussion, gives helpful tips on group dynamics and suggests ways to deal with problems which may arise during the discussion. With such helps, someone with little or no experience can lead an effective group study.

Suggestions for Individual Study
1. As you begin the study, pray that God will help you understand the passage and apply it to your life. Ask him to show you what kinds of action to take as a result of your time of study.
2. In your first session take time to read the introduction to the entire guide. This will orient you to the subject at hand and to the author's goals for the studies.
3. Read the short introduction to the study.
4. Read and reread the suggested Bible passage to familiarize yourself with it.

5. A good modern translation of the Bible will give you the most help. The New International Version, the New American Standard Bible and the New Revised Standard Version are all recommended. The questions in this guide are based on the New International Version.

6. Use the space provided to jot your answers to the questions. This will help you express your understanding of the passage clearly.

7. Take time with the final questions and the "Respond" section in each study to commit yourself to action and/or a change in attitude. You may wish to find a study partner to discuss your insights with, one who will keep you accountable for the commitments you make.

Suggestions for Members of a Group Study

1. Come to the study prepared. Follow the suggestions for individual study mentioned above. You will find that careful preparation will greatly enrich your time spent in group discussion.

2. Be willing to participate in the discussion. The leader of your group will not be lecturing. Instead, he or she will be encouraging the members of the group to discuss what they have learned. The leader will be asking the questions that are found in this guide.

3. Stick to the topic being discussed. Your answers should be based on the verses which are the focus of the discussion.

4. Be sensitive to the other members of the group. Listen attentively when they describe what they have learned. You may be surprised by their insights! When possible, link what you say to the comments of others. Also, be affirming whenever you can. This will encourage some of the more hesitant members of the group to participate.

5. Be careful not to dominate the discussion. We are sometimes so eager to express our thoughts that we leave too little opportunity for others to respond. By all means participate! But allow others to do so as well.

6. Expect God to teach you through the passage being discussed and through the other members of the group. Pray that you will have an enjoyable and profitable time together, but also that as a result of the study you will find ways you can take action individually and/or as a group.

7. Be ready to make a personal application of the principles in the study. The final questions will guide you in this. Although you may or may not wish to discuss the "Respond" section as a group, you may want to hold one another accountable in some way for those personal commitments. **8.** We recommend that groups agree to follow a few basic guidelines, and that these be read at the beginning of the first session. You may wish to adapt the following guidelines to your situation:

☐ Anything personal which is shared in the group is considered confidential and will not be discussed outside the group unless specific permission is given to do so.

☐ We will provide time for each person present to talk if he or she feels comfortable doing so.

☐ We will talk about ourselves and our own situations, avoiding conversation about other people.

☐ We will listen attentively to each other.

☐ We will be very cautious about giving advice.

☐ We will pray for each other.

If you are the group leader, you will find additional suggestions at the back of the guide.

How the Series Works

Where should you start? If you'd like to go through several guides in the series, whether with a group or individually, a good place to start is *Sexual Wholeness.* This guide will give you a good overview of the issues, and you may find various areas you want to explore further. While *Sexual Wholeness* may be used in either same-sex or mixed (male and female) groups, it may be uncomfortable for some in mixed groups. As a companion to that guide, you may wish to use *Created for Relationships.* If you are in a mixed group, this may be a more comfortable starting place.

Created Female and *Created Male* are designed for same-sex groups but could be used together for enlightening discussions in mixed groups. To facilitate this use, studies three through five are the same in both guides. The other studies could be intermixed so that group members have a unique opportunity to hear the perspective, needs and struggles of the other sex.

Women Facing Temptation and _Men Facing Temptation_ are also designed for same-sex groups but could be adapted for use in mixed groups. You will find that all the temptations covered are applicable to either gender. This could be an opportunity for interesting discussion about how these temptations are both similar and distinct for each sex. You may discover new ways to support each other and help one another avoid temptation.

For two quarters of study on how we live out our gender roles, _Roles in Ministry_ and _Following God Together_ make good study companions. _Roles in Ministry_ looks specifically at the role of women in the church by studying the relevant passages and is designed to help the reader find a unique place of service. Through a series of character studies involving pairs of men and women, _Following God Together_ will help us see the temptations and frustrations men and women find in service together and the great possibilities for ministry when abilities are combined.

Introducing *Roles in Ministry*

The question of how male-female roles in the church should be structured has become a volatile one in recent years. The issue centers around what kinds of responsibilities are appropriate for women. Can women teach? Can women preach? Can women be deacons? elders? Should women be ordained ministers?

The questions get bigger and bigger, calling into question everything from our gender roles to how we receive salvation.

The Traditional View

In a *Christianity Today* article J. I. Packer makes the following plea:

Oxford has been called the home of lost causes, and here am I, an Oxford man, pleading for an end to something that is now standard practice in Methodist, Baptist, Lutheran, Congregational, Pentecostal and Presbyterian denominations, along with the Anglican churches of the U.S.A., Canada, New Zealand, and Ireland. Is this a lost cause?

Packer goes on to list four major reasons he thinks women should not be made presbyters—that is, priests or elders. He refers to the authority of Scripture, particularly 1 Timothy 2:11, and to the fact that Christ is male. He also looks to the roles which were set forth at creation, with the man leading and the woman serving as his helper. Finally, he notes the example of Mary as the model woman who served faithfully without ordination. Packer concludes:

What has been said highlights the reason why women seek the presbyterate (they have gifts for ministry and a sense of pastoral vocation, and no lesser role offers them the scope they desire); but it also highlights the reason why ordaining them to that office is inappropriate (Scripture presents presbyteral leadership as a man's job). In practice, ordaining women presbyters has regularly proved divisive without being particularly fruitful—a state of affairs that may be expected to continue. What wisdom is there in pushing ahead with this policy? None that I can see.[1]

The Egalitarian View

In her talk at an evangelical colloquium on women, Patricia Gundry read the following letter, which describes how one woman has suffered because of the limitations put on her.

It wasn't too long ago that I cried myself to sleep because of an excess accumulation of church-dispensed propaganda on the inferiority of women (oppression in the name of Christ, I call it). I was so devastated that I was beginning to almost believe the Holy Spirit in me was somehow not the same Holy Spirit that indwelled "the brethren," or if otherwise, why am I to keep quiet in the church and not let that Holy Spirit speak through me, simply because I have a woman's body? God surely makes more sense than that. But they pointed to the Holy Scripture for "proof" and I was about to sink under it. "Bring your pies, ladies, but leave your ideas at home."[2]

Gundry continues, "I was very conscious of my silent sisters while I began my first book, and I remained conscious of them throughout its production. I knew there were thousands, probably millions, who wanted answers to the same questions I had. But they were afraid to ask, embarrassed to pursue the first rebuffs, or they didn't know whom to ask. But they wanted so much to know."[3]

Deciding for Yourself

During this study, it will be okay for you to ask questions—hard questions—of yourself and of others. You'll work through the relevant passages and have an opportunity to respond with your own thoughts and opinions. And you'll consider the issues from a variety of perspectives.

At the end of the study I hope you will have a clear idea of how you think roles in the church should work. More important, I hope you will be convinced that *you* have a role in church. We are all, male and female alike, called to be ministers of Christ's love.

What is God calling you to do?

Cindy Bunch

---

[1] J. I. Packer, "Let's Stop Making Women Presbyters," *Christianity Today*, February 11, 1991, pp. 18-21.
[2] Patricia Gundry, "Why We're Here," in *Women, Authority and the Bible*, ed. Alvera Mickelsen (Downers Grove, Ill.: InterVarsity Press, 1986), p. 14.
[3] Ibid., p. 16.

1
Created in God's Image

Genesis 1:26-31

*T*he day he found out that the adoption agency had a child for us, your father smiled all the way home from work. As a matter of fact, he looked so happy that a man on the subway asked him why he was smiling. And people on the subway in Philadelphia never speak to anyone!"

This is how my mother described the feelings she and my father had about my birth. I was a child when she told me this story, but her joy was so great even in the retelling that I still remember her words many years later.

Such was the joy of God the Father when he created men and women.

Open
Think about a birth which you have experienced. It could be the birth of your own child. Or it could be a time when you have been with close friends or relatives soon after their baby was born.

☐ Describe what you [the parents] were like.

☐ What kinds of things were said about the baby?

☐ If you had the opportunity, what would you tell that child about the day of his or her birth?

Study
Read Genesis 1:26-31.
1. What do you think the birth of humanity was like for God the Father?

2. Think over what you know about God. What is God like?

3. What, then, does it mean that God created us in his own image?

4. How does the fact that you are created in God's image affect how you feel about yourself?

How does it affect the way you feel about the other sex?

5. God doesn't *need* humanity in order to exist. God has everything he needs within himself. Why do you think God created humanity?

6. God further invests in humanity by giving us great responsibilities. What does he command the first human beings to do?

7. God describes his creation as "very good." What implications does this have for how we understand ourselves and our world?

8. How does this passage affect what you see as the role of the opposite sex in God's created world?

Respond
During the next week, make an effort to look at the people around you as individuals who are created uniquely. Concentrate on someone you don't like; view him or her as being created in God's image. At the end of the week take time to reflect on how your thinking has changed.

2
God's Good Gift

Genesis 2:18-25

W inter, spring, summer or fall—all you have to do is call. And I'll be there. Yes, I will. You've got a friend."

These words from James Taylor's "You've Got a Friend" always remind me of my friend Carrie. We don't live close together, but she is faithful about sending cards and letters. Often, just knowing that she is thinking about me, and that she cares about my life, is all I need to get through a hard day.

Relationships are a great gift from God.

Open

Think about a time when you felt really alone. Describe how a friend or spouse helped you through such a time by sending you a card, cooking you a meal, listening, praying with you or offering some other form of comfort.

Study

Read Genesis 2:18-25.

1. In verse 18 God says, "It is not good for the man to be alone." Why do you think God says this?

2. How is the woman different from the other animals?

3. The Hebrew word for helper (vv. 18, 20) is the same as that in Psalm 121:1-2: "I lift my eyes to the hills—where does my help come from? My help comes from the LORD, the Maker of heaven and earth." What does this tell you about what God has in mind when he talks about a helper for the man?

4. How do you respond to the idea of the woman being a "suitable helper"?

5. What significance do you see in the man's naming of the woman (v. 23)?

6. What is the symbolic meaning of the man and woman being "one flesh"?

7. What does this passage tell you about the role of a man?

8. What do you see as the role of the woman as helper today?

9. How does your view of men's and women's roles affect how you do ministry?

Respond
Whether you are male or female, during the next week take time to reflect on how you live out your created role.

3
Fallen Together

Genesis 3:1-6

W hat does the Bible say about the sins of women? One woman puts it this way: "We eat apples, we look back, we seduce God's chosen"[1]—referring to the sins of Eve, Lot's wife and Delilah.

What about men? In the biblical stories of Adam, Lot and Goliath we see how men are tempted. Men also eat apples when instructed otherwise. Men get drunk. And men have affairs.

We are all vulnerable to the effects of the Fall.

Open
The following are some common temptations that men and women face:

Lust	Competition	Bitterness	Anger
Jealousy	Blaming	Gossip	Fear
Materialism	Independence	Coveting	Controlling
Manipulation	Discontentment	Performing	Hiding
Passivity	Dependence	Overeating	Pleasing

☐ Which of these do you associate particularly with men?

with women?

☐ Discuss why you see these differences in how we are most easily tempted.

Study
Read Genesis 3:1-6.
1. Look through the passage, and cite the times deceit takes place.

2. How does the serpent distort God's words in verse 1? (See Genesis 2:16-17.)

3. How does the woman add to God's command (v. 3) and what does this tell us about her?

4. How does the serpent tempt the woman in verses 4-5?

5. According to verse 6, for what reasons does the woman take the fruit?

6. The man accepts the fruit from the woman. Verse 6 tells us that he has been with her the whole time. What do you think he has been thinking and doing during this dialogue?

7. Why do you think the man never spoke up?

8. What do you see as the man's responsibility in this event?

the woman's?

Respond
Think about ways in which you allow the sin of deceit to get hold of you. Notice particularly the subtle process of rationalizing which your mind goes through as you are tempted. Confess this before the Lord and ask him to make his presence known to you.

---

[1]Mary Cartledge-Hayes, *To Love Delilah* (San Diego, Calif.: LuraMedia, 1990), p. 14.

4
Accepting Responsibility

Genesis 3:7-19

I was a model child. As the eldest, I was quite mature and responsible—even at a young age. However, one evening I fell prey to the ever-present "crayon" temptation. Just as many other children before and after me have, I scribbled on the wall.

When my mother asked me who had colored on the wall, I of course pointed at my two-year-old brother. He was too young to defend himself, so I was off the hook.

At one time or another, we've all wrongly placed blame on others and failed to accept responsibility for our actions. Unfortunately, the sin and its consequence are often much more serious than scribbling on a wall.

Open

☐ What does being a responsible person involve?

☐ How is responsibility a part of the Christian life?

Study

Read Genesis 3:7-19.

1. Looking through this passage, what results of sin do you see?

2. Genesis 2:25 says, "The man and his wife were both naked, and they felt no shame." Why does this change in verse 7?

3. Of course God knew where they were. Why do you think he asks the question in verse 9?

4. How does the man respond to God's next questions (vv. 11-12)?

5. What is the woman's response to God's question (v. 13)?

6. God makes the woman and the serpent enemies (v. 15). What significance do you see in this curse for today?

7. In what ways is the woman cursed?

the man?

8. Describe the effects of the curse on the relationship between husband and wife (v. 16).

Respond

Allow God's voice to ask, "Where are you?"

Reflect on how you have recently placed blame on another person and failed to accept your responsibility. Confess your sin silently or to others whom you trust, and pray for forgiveness and healing in that relationship. Think about whether taking responsibility means you need to go to the person and ask forgiveness.

5
Freedom in Christ

Galatians 3:26-28

*P*rejudice comes in many forms. It might be a reaction to a physical attribute—a nose that's considered too large, an early bald spot, buck teeth. It can be focused on any nationality or ethnic group in the minority. Religion, politics, social class, and gender are all possible areas of discrimination.

Christ came to break down the barriers that prejudice creates and to bring us together as the family of God.

Open

☐ What are the advantages of being a woman in the church?

the advantages of being a man?

☐ What are the disadvantages of being a woman in the church?

the disadvantages of being a man?

Study
Read Galatians 3:26-28.
1. Describe what it means to be clothed with Christ. (How does such a person look? feel? act?)

2. The Galatians were arguing over the role of the law in their salvation. In this passage Paul is showing them why they should have unity. What is the significance of the fact that they are all baptized in Christ?

3. What contrasts are made in verse 28?

4. What generalizations can you make from the contrasts Paul sets up?

5. From what you know about Paul's culture, how would this have been a particularly radical statement?

6. What does it mean to be Abraham's seed (v. 29)?

7. How do these verses help you to understand roles in the church?

8. How does this view encourage you specifically in your ministry (or challenge you to get involved in ministry)?

Respond
Your life should reflect the fact that you are a child of God. Does it? This week, be aware that you are free in Christ and try to let that freedom show.

6
Women Led Astray

2 Timothy 3:1-9

Wen life becomes painful, even overwhelming, people often become more open to spiritual matters. For example, Manuel Noriega is said to have had a born-again experience while in prison. However, just as people who are spiritually needy are open to the gospel, so are they vulnerable to cults and false teachers. This study explores the results of such unions.

Open
☐ How have you seen people in the church led astray?

☐ Why do you think those people were particularly vulnerable in that situation?

☐ How could you be a help in such situations?

Study
Read 2 Timothy 3:1-9.
1. Paul explicitly describes the characteristics of godless people in verses 2-5. What word or phrase do you think best describes them? Why?

Does anything in this list surprise you?

2. What does it mean to have a "form" of godliness?

3. Why are women particularly vulnerable to these false teachers (vv. 6-7)?

4. According to Jewish tradition, Jannes and Jambres were Egyptian court magicians who opposed Moses when he performed miracles before Pharaoh. What does this comparison tell you about the false teachers?

5. Paul says they won't get far because "their folly will be evident to everyone" (v. 9), yet earlier we see that some women are being swayed by them. What sort of person would be likely to see through these teachers?

6. Do you think women are particularly vulnerable to false teaching today? Why or why not?

Respond
Be aware of people around you who are spiritually vulnerable. If you think a person is open to hearing about God, then tell him or her about the truth that sets us free.

7
Unity in Worship

1 Timothy 2:1-15

I was at the Urbana 90 InterVarsity Missions Conference. We were singing songs of praise to the Lord—each verse in a different language. From my seat I could see Christians from all around the world worshiping the Lord. That was a worship experience I will never forget.

When we worship together, God's Spirit can work with great power to unite us. Unfortunately, sometimes we get caught up in superficial debates which divide us at the very time we should come together. In this study we will look at a church which was struggling with these issues.

. . . and I got that scar from the chairman of the Ladies' Aid Society during the second battle of "Guitars in the Sanctuary" back in '71.

Open

☐ The cartoon above illustrates how we allow physical details to get in the way of worshiping the Lord. What kinds of issues surrounding worship divide your church?

☐ Describe a worship service which was particularly meaningful to you and tell what made it so special.

Study

Read 1 Timothy 2:1-15.

1. Looking through this passage, what do you think is Paul's purpose in teaching on worship? Why?

2. In verse 8 the Greek does not refer to humanity but to men. Why do you think these instructions are given specifically to males?

3. Some Christian groups take verse 9 quite literally. How would you apply verses 9-10?

4. Verses 11-12 have been the root of a great deal of debate between faithful Christians. What do you believe to be the purpose of this teaching?

5. Verses 13-14 interpret the creation story. How do these verses fit into your understanding of the creation and the Fall?

6. Verse 5 tells us that there is only one mediator, yet verse 15 says "women will be saved through childbearing." How do you understand these verses in relation to each other?

7. At the end of verse 15, Paul says that women should "continue in faith, love and holiness with propriety." How does this sentence provide a summary of his teaching on worship throughout the passage?

Respond
Consider how you could experience greater unity in the church and/or fellowship where you worship. Take steps to bring unity to that setting.

8
Interdependence

1 Corinthians 11:3-16

*S*ociety tells us that we should look out for ourselves. We learn to value independence above all else. But it is not a Christian value. Scripture says that we were created for each other—not to be dependent on each other in an unhealthy way, but to be interdependent.

Open
☐ Which of the following advertising slogans best describes how you view the authority structure between men and women? Explain your choice.

"Strength in Numbers" (The Equitable)

"The New Generation" (Oldsmobile)

"Quality Is Job 1" (Ford)

"Accept No Limitations" (Minolta)

"I Love What You Do for Me" (Toyota)

"You Deserve a Break Today" (McDonald's)

"The Real Thing" (Coke)

"There's No Substitute for Experience" (Honda)

"You've Come a Long Way, Baby" (Virginia Slims)

Study

Read 1 Corinthians 11:3-16.

1. Paul sets up an organizing structure in verse 3. Describe it in your own words.

2. How have you seen this structure effectively and/or ineffectively applied?

3. Why is it important for a man to have his head uncovered when prophesying (vv. 4, 7)?

4. What does it mean for a woman to have her head covered when praying (vv. 6, 8-10)?

5. According to verses 7-10, what are the differences between men and women?

6. How do verses 11-12 help you to understand the whole passage?

7. In verses 14-15 Paul uses a highly subjective "natural" argument to defend his point that women should have their heads covered. How does that affect your understanding of this passage?

8. How do you apply this teaching today?

Respond

In what ways are women in your church involved in worship? Consider whether this accurately reflects what you believe Scripture teaches. Talk to others to find out what they think about women's roles in worship.

9
Requirements for Leaders

1 Timothy 3:1-13

*S*ome churches have deacons. Some have elders. Some have both. The Baptist church I grew up in had neither. We had a church board with committee chairpersons who led the church.

Whatever their titles, the leaders of the church are vital to the life of the church. The Bible gives us specific qualifications for selecting godly leaders.

Open
☐ What are the key qualities a male leader should have?

☐ What qualities should a female leader have?

☐ If you saw differences between what a male and a female leader should be like, explain why.

Study
Read 1 Timothy 3:1-13.
1. From verses 1-7, summarize in your own words the character and lifestyle of an overseer (elder).

2. Verse 4 emphasizes family life. Why do you think it is important to look at a leader's family?

3. Why would a recent convert be particularly vulnerable to temptation?

4. What traits are emphasized for deacons (vv. 8-9)?

5. What is faith with a clear conscience like?

6. An NIV text note suggests that "their wives" might also be translated "deaconesses." Clearly, these women were serving in the church in some way. Why would the traits listed in verse 11 be important for these women to have?

7. Throughout the passage, the leader's marriage is emphasized. What are some ways a leader's spouse can help or hinder ministry?

8. In study 12 we will read about Phoebe, who is described as a "deaconess" (Romans 16:1), and verse 11 may refer to deaconesses, but this passage focuses on men who are deacons and elders. Do you think this passage excludes women from leadership as deacons and elders? Why or why not?

Respond
Find out more about your church's policy on selecting elders and deacons. Why qualifications are looked for? Are women included in these roles? Why or why not?

10
The "Proper" Role

Luke 10:38-42

W hen are you going to fix the toaster?" said the bride to her new husband.

"How do I put this diaper on the baby?" the new father asked his wife.

Society assumes that men will be able to change the oil in the car and fix small appliances. Women are expected to know how to cook and care for children. These stereotyped roles are unfortunate, however, because they limit both sexes. When we are unable to break out of convention, we often miss out on doing things which we are good at and enjoy.

Open
☐ What are some typical ways you see women involved in ministry?

☐ In what ways do you often see men involved in ministry?

☐ Do you think it is important that men's and women's ministries remain distinct? Why or why not?

Study
Read Luke 10:38-42.
1. Jewish men rarely spent time talking with their wives and never spoke to other women. Why do you think Jesus was talking with Mary and Martha?

2. What potential risks would this have created for Jesus' ministry?

3. What does the fact that Martha "opened her home" to Jesus say about her?

4. Mary is listening to Jesus while Martha prepares hospitality for him. What kinds of expectations does Martha's complaint in verse 40 reveal?

5. How does Jesus respond?

6. What do you think Jesus means when he says "only one thing is needed"?

7. Do you think women today are making the choices Jesus wants them to? Explain.

8. Explain how you are more like Mary or Martha.

Which do you want to be? Why?

Respond

Thank God for the gifts he has given you. Ask him to give you the courage to always follow his voice and not allow others to force their preconceived notions on you.

11
Ministering Together

Acts 18:18-28

*M*y friend Kim is a drug rehabilitation counselor who works with troubled teens. Her husband, Robert, is a youth pastor. I was visiting them the night a teenage girl called and asked for help. I went with them to meet her at the bus station.

This girl was obviously in trouble, but she was also clearly lying to us about her past. Kim was able to draw her story out, asking tough questions when necessary. Robert was able to help her spiritually, explaining the gospel and what it requires of us in a way she could understand.

That night, I saw how the Lord was using the unique gifts of this husband and wife to create a powerful team.

Open
☐ Describe a couple who has ministered to you.

☐ What were their different gifts?

☐ How did they complement each other?

Study
Read Acts 18:18-28.
1. From this passage what do you think Priscilla and Aquila were like?

2. In New Testament times it was expected that the man's name would appear first when a husband and wife were listed. Why do you think Priscilla's name appears first here?

3. What do we learn about Apollos in verses 24-25?

4. What did Apollos know about Jesus?

5. What do you think the conversation between Apollos and Priscilla and Aquila was like? Describe it.

6. How does their teaching appear to have affected Apollos (vv. 27-28)?

7. How does this passage help you understand the roles of men and women in the church?

Respond

Take time to write or call the couple you mentioned in the opening, to thank them for their ministry to you. Find out more about how God has used them in ministry together.

12
Many Workers

Romans 16:1-16

*E*very Sunday morning when I enter my church, Nora Mae greets me with a warm smile and words of welcome. Carol and Jan often help take the offering or serve Communion during the service. Kathy, a seminary student, helps lead worship, gives the children's sermon and sometimes preaches. Holly encourages us all with her beautiful singing. And Betty and Jane are often at work in the kitchen, serving special meals.

Each of these women is uniquely gifted for the ministry of the church. But are all of these roles appropriate for them?

Open

☐ The following are the four views which are represented in *Women in Ministry: Four Views* (IVP). These are the most common ways of understanding the Scriptures we have been studying. Examine these views and choose the one which best fits your beliefs. Then give several reasons for your choice.

Traditional: Let your women keep silence. Women are not to be involved in ministry.

Male leadership: The head of the woman is the man. Women can have limited involvement as long as they are under the direction of a male pastor.

Plural ministry: Your sons and your daughters shall prophesy. All believers are ministers, but the role of the minister should be modified. Overemphasizing ordination creates arguments over women's roles.

Egalitarian: There is neither male nor female in Christ. Women should engage in any kind of service for which they are gifted and to which they feel called.

Study
Read Romans 16:1-16.
1. Look through the passage and note the number of times Paul mentions women.

2. From these verses what kind of person do you think Phoebe was?

3. The NIV translation for verse 1 reads "servant," but a text note suggests "deaconess" is another possible translation. What does Phoebe's role in the church appear to have been?

4. What do we learn about Priscilla and Aquila in verses 3-5?

5. Looking through verses 6-15, note ways in which the people mentioned here have served Christ.

6. In what ways have they served Paul?

7. What kinds of things are said about them?

8. What would you like for people to say about your ministry in the church?

Respond
We need all kinds of people working in our churches. Whether you are male or female, get involved in a ministry you feel is appropriate to your understanding of your role and gifts.

Guidelines for Leaders

Leading a Bible discussion can be an enjoyable and rewarding experience. But it can also be intimidating—especially if you've never done it before. If this is how you feel, you're in good company.

Remember when God asked Moses to lead the Israelites out of Egypt? Moses replied, "O Lord, please send someone else to do it" (Exodus 4:13). But God gave Moses the help (human and divine) he needed to be a strong leader.

Leading a Bible discussion is not difficult if you follow certain guidelines. You don't need to be an expert on the Bible or a trained teacher. The suggestions listed below can help you to effectively fulfill your role as leader—and enjoy doing it.

Preparing for the Study

1. As you study the passage ahead of time, ask God to help you understand it and apply it in your own life. Unless this happens, you will not be prepared to lead others. Pray too for the various members of the group. Ask God to open your hearts to the message of his Word and motivate you to action.

2. Read the introduction to the entire guide to get an overview of the subject at hand and the issues which will be explored.

3. Be ready for the "Open" questions with a personal story or example.

The group will be only as vulnerable and open as its leader.

4. As you begin preparing for each study, read and reread the assigned Bible passage to familiarize yourself with it.

5. This study guide is based on the New International Version of the Bible. It will help you and the group if you use this translation as the basis for your study and discussion.

6. Carefully work through each question in the study. Spend time in meditation and reflection as you consider how to respond.

7. Write your thoughts and responses in the space provided in the study guide. This will help you to express your understanding of the passage clearly.

8. It might help you to have a Bible dictionary handy. Use it to look up any unfamiliar words, names or places. (For additional help on how to study a passage, see chapter five of *Leading Bible Discussions,* IVP.)

9. Take the final (application) questions and the "Respond" portion of each study seriously. Consider what this means for your life—what changes you may need to make in your lifestyle and/or actions you can take in your church or with people you know. Remember that the group will follow your lead in responding to the studies.

Leading the Study

1. Be sure everyone in your group has a study guide and Bible. Encourage the group to prepare beforehand for each discussion by reading the introduction to the guide and by working through the questions in the study.

2. At the beginning of your first time together, explain that these studies are meant to be discussions, not lectures. Encourage the members of the group to participate. However, do not put pressure on those who may be hesitant to speak during the first few sessions.

3. Begin the study on time. Open with prayer, asking God to help the group understand and apply the passage.

4. Have a group member read the introductory paragraph at the beginning of the discussion. This will remind the group of the topic of the study.

5. Every study begins with a section called "Open." These "approach" questions are meant to be asked before the passage is read. They are important for several reasons.

First, there is always a stiffness that needs to be overcome before people will begin to talk openly. A good question will break the ice.

Second, most people will have lots of different things going on in their minds (dinner, an exam, an important meeting coming up, how to get the car fixed) that have nothing to do with the study. A creative question will get their attention and draw them into the discussion.

Third, approach questions can reveal where our thoughts or feelings need to be transformed by Scripture. That is why it is especially important not to read the passage before the approach question is asked. The passage will tend to color the honest reactions people would otherwise give, because they feel they are supposed to think the way the Bible does.

6. Have a group member read aloud the passage to be studied.

7. As you ask the questions, keep in mind that they are designed to be used just as they are written. You may simply read them aloud. Or you may prefer to express them in your own words.

There may be times when it is appropriate to deviate from the study guide. For example, a question may already have been answered. If so, move on to the next question. Or someone may raise an important question not covered in the guide. Take time to discuss it, but try to keep the group from going off on tangents.

8. Avoid answering your own questions. Repeat or rephrase them if necessary until they are clearly understood. An eager group quickly becomes passive and silent if members think the leader will give all the "right" answers.

9. Don't be afraid of silence. People may need time to think about the question before formulating their answers.

10. Don't be content with just one answer. Ask "What do the rest of you think?" or "Anything else?" until several people have given answers to a question.

11. Acknowledge all contributions. Be affirming whenever possible. Never reject an answer. If it is clearly off base, ask "Which verse led you to that conclusion?" or "What do the rest of you think?"

12. Don't expect every answer to be addressed to you, even though this will probably happen at first. As group members become more at ease, they will begin to truly interact with each other. This is one sign of healthy discussion.

13. Don't be afraid of controversy. It can be stimulating! If you don't resolve an issue completely, don't be frustrated. Move on and keep it in mind for later. A subsequent study may solve the problem.

14. Periodically summarize what the group has said about the passage. This helps to draw together the various ideas mentioned and gives continuity to the study. But don't preach.

15. Don't skip over the application questions at the end of each study. It's important that we each apply the message of the passage to ourselves in a specific way. Be willing to get things started by describing how you have been affected by the study.

Depending on the makeup of your group and the length of time you've been together, you may or may not want to discuss the "Respond" section. If not, allow the group to read it and reflect on it silently. Encourage members to make specific commitments and to write them in their study guide. Ask them the following week how they did with their commitments.

16. Conclude your time together with conversational prayer. Ask for God's help in following through on the commitments you've made.

17. End on time.

Many more suggestions and helps are found in *The Big Book on Small Groups, Small Group Leaders' Handbook* and *Good Things Come in Small Groups* (IVP). Reading through one of these books would be worth your time.

Study Notes

Study 1. Created in God's Image. Genesis 1:26-31.
Purpose: To understand who it is that God created us to be and find our self-worth in that.

Question 3. Because we are all created in God's image, we are all to be treated with respect and honor. Each of us is unique and valuable. And we are capable of sharing the characteristics of God, such as righteousness and holiness.

Question 4. The fact that we are created in God's image should give us confidence in our abilities and freedom to reflect God's image in its completeness. We should not limit our options—or those of others. God gives us freedom to explore the world and all its possibilities.

Question 5. God's great love cannot be contained. It must overflow in creative channels. God's work of creating humanity provided satisfaction within itself. Like an artist or a painter, God *must* create. Additionally, God, as we understand him through the doctrine of the Trinity, is by definition in relationship. The creation of humanity is an extension of God's desire to be in relationship.

Question 7. "Everything God created is good (see vv. 10, 12, 18, 21, 25). . . . The creation, as fashioned and ordered by God, has no lingering traces of disorder and no dark and threatening forces. . . . Even darkness and the deep were given benevolent functions in a world fashioned to bless and sustain life" (*The NIV Study Bible,* Kenneth Barker, gen. ed. [Grand Rapids, Mich.: Zondervan, 1985], p. 6).

Study 2. God's Good Gift. Genesis 2:18-25.

Purpose: To understand why God created two sexes and how he intended for us to relate to one another.

General note. This passage is critical to our understanding of who we are as men and women in God's image. If you have studied *Created for Relationships* or *Sexual Wholeness,* you will have studied this passage there. The study has been slightly reworked to help you focus on the theme of roles in ministry, so you may want to study the passage again to see what God reveals to you on this topic. Or, if you wish, you can move on to the next study.

Question 1. "Without female companionship and a partner in reproduction, the man could not fully realize his humanity" (*The NIV Study Bible,* p. 9). Even if we are not married, we share life with friends and companions of both sexes. Paul Jewett has said, "Humanity that is not shared is inhumanity. . . . Shared humanity is what it is because Man is like God" (*Man as Male and Female* [Grand Rapids, Mich.: Eerdmans, 1975], p. 36).

Question 2. One possible response is that the woman is created more like the man, while the animals are considerably different from the man. Consider the implications for this in our relationships with each other.

Most English translations begin verse 19 with "So God . . ." or "So out of the ground God . . ." This seems to imply that the animals were created after the man, and specifically as potential partners for the man. This account from chapter 2 is noticeably different from chapter 1. Some readers may not have been aware of this and may be surprised to read that the man was created before the animals. It is tempting to dwell on the differences between the two accounts. However, the important point to remember is that each story has its own purpose. The focus in chapter 2 is more on the humans than in chapter 1; also, chapter 2 is continued in chapters 3-4.

Question 3. Some may read these verses as calling for a hierarchical relationship, drawing on Ephesians 5:21-33. Others disagree, calling for egalitarian roles:

> The Hebrew word *ezer* (translated "helper"), according to Berkeley and Alvera Mickelsen, does not imply subordination. It is used in other cases to describe God as our "helper" (Ps 20:2; 33:20; 70:5; 115:9-11; 121:1-2; 124:8). Eve was made of the "same stuff" as Adam so that he at once recognized her as just like himself. She was a helper 'fit for him' (Gen 2:18 RSV). The word *fit* can be translated "equal and corresponding to." (Kari Torjesen Malcolm, *Women at the Crossroads* [Downers Grove, Ill.: InterVarsity Press, 1982], p. 156)

It should also be noted that several translations use *partner* instead of *helper.*

Question 5. *The NIV Study Bible* points out that "in ancient times, to name something or someone implied having dominion or ownership" (p. 6). Do you think this has any implications for the relationship between the man and the woman?

On the other hand, an NIV text note points out that the "Hebrew for *woman* sounds like the Hebrew for *man.*" This would suggest that in giving her a name similar to his own, the man recognized her as someone like himself—a partner.

Questions 7-8. Opinions on the role of the man and the woman will vary greatly depending on church and family background and opinions about how key biblical texts are interpreted. Some may see very distinct role patterns while others may think that there are no differences. There are no "right" answers here. Each person should be encouraged to talk about his or her biblical and theological convictions.

Study 3. Fallen Together. Genesis 3:1-6.

Purpose: To explore the implications of the Fall and understand the role of both sexes in that event.

Question 3. God's command in Genesis 2:16-17 does not say that they cannot *touch* the tree, yet the woman adds that as she repeats God's instructions. This is our first clue that the woman is being swayed by the serpent's logic.

Question 6. Often blame for the Fall is placed on the woman, who actively sinned. It is important to recognize, however, that even before he took the fruit, the man sinned in his passivity. You may want to read the following retelling of this story to your group to get a different perspective on what happened:

"Leave my apples alone," God said.

"Okay," said the first couple. . . .

One day Adam and Eve went for a walk. They planned to turn left at the apple tree, but, as sometimes happens, they stopped to talk to an acquaintance and got sidetracked.

"Want an apple?" said the snake.

"Oh, gee, I don't know," said Eve. "I really shouldn't. What do you think, Adam?"

Adam didn't say a word.

"Oh, come on," said the snake. "It'll be a whole new taste sensation. Give it a shot."

"Shall I, Adam?"

Adam didn't say a word.

"What can it hurt?" asked the snake.

Eve took the apple.

Adam didn't say a word.

Eve bit into the apple.

Adam didn't say a word.

"Yummy," said Eve. "Adam, would you like a bite?"

"Yes, thanks," said Adam.

And he too ate from the apple. (Mary Cartledge-Hayes, *To Love Delilah,* pp. 17-18)

Question 8. Susan Foh, an advocate of male leadership, says that verse 16, "Your desire will be for your husband, and he shall rule over you," really means that "Eve's desire was to dominate or control her husband." Alvera Mickelsen, an egalitarian, points out that the "text never suggests this." She adds, "The term *desire* comes in context of childbearing. Childbirth does not usually result from a wife's desire to dominate her husband! The common-sense reading points to her longing for her pre-Fall intimate harmony with her husband" ("An Egalitarian View" in *Women in Ministry,* ed. Bonnidell Clouse and Robert G. Clouse [Downers Grove, Ill.: InterVarsity Press, 1989], p. 186).

Study 4. Accepting Responsibility. Genesis 3:7-19.
Purpose: To explore the impact of the Fall on how men and women relate to each other.
Question 1. We can see shame (v. 7), withdrawal from God (v. 8), fear (v. 10), blame (v. 12, 13), enmity (v. 15), pain (vv. 16-17), and death (v. 19).
Question 3. Perhaps God intended for the question to cause them to think about how their actions affected their relationship with him. God was asking where they were in relation to him.

Study 5. Freedom in Christ. Galatians 3:26-28.
Purpose: To explore how we have been set free from gender distinctions in Christ.
Question 2. "In baptism, each person is stripped of any dignity due him or her and reclothed with the sole dignity of Christ. . . . Being baptized into Christ institutes a new value system in which religious, social and sexual differences do not play a part" (Klyne R. Snodgrass, "Galatians 3:28: Conundrum or Solution?" in *Women, Authority & the Bible,* ed. Alvera Mickelsen [Downers Grove, Ill.: InterVarsity Press, 1986], pp. 174-75).
Question 3. Verse 28 touches on racial, social and sexual differences.
Question 4. With regard to gender, the statement is radical. "The standing of a woman in the Christian community is not linked to a man; she, like every man, has her standing only because of Christ and, like every man, she as an individual partakes of the new unity in Christ. Being in Christ does not change a woman into a man any more than it changes Gentiles into Jews, but it changes the way that men and women relate to each other just as it changed the way Jews and Gentiles relate" (Klyne R. Snodgrass, "Galatians 3:28," p. 177).
Question 5. "Galatians 3:28 *is* the most socially explosive text in the New Testament, and if given its due, it will confront and change our lives and communities" (Klyne R. Snodgrass, "Galatians 3:28," pp. 167-68).

For example, "Paul's thought with regard to slavery is much more revolutionary than is usually acknowledged, even with the house codes attempting to redefine what it meant to be a slave. That Paul could ask Philemon to receive Onesimus back as a brother *both in the flesh and in the Lord* (v. 16) shows how seriously the words of Galatians 3:28 should be taken" (Klyne R. Snodgrass, "Galatians 3:28," p. 176).

Question 7. According to Snodgrass, "Paul obviously did not give up on the idea of hierarchy, and I would argue that equality and hierarchy are not necessarily antithetical ideas. Nevertheless, what did change for Paul and must change for every Christian is the understanding of hierarchy. Christianity redefines hierarchy in terms of love, servanthood and mutual submission. If the new age has broken in, we cannot allow ourselves to continue to be determined by the old. Only Christ can legitimately determine our existence and our relationships" ("Galatians 3:28," p. 175).

Study 6. Women Led Astray. 2 Timothy 3:1-9.
Purpose: To look at the cultural situation surrounding Paul's injunction to women not to teach.

Question 3. Verse 6 says that they are "weak-willed," feeling guilty because of their sins, and "swayed by evil desires." Verse 7 suggests that they probably had been taught about Christ (they knew enough about sin to feel guilt) but never acted on that teaching in their lives. It is also important to remember that women at this time did not receive much formal education. Thus, they would have been more vulnerable to false teaching.

"According to 1 Timothy 5, among these women are some younger widows who 'live for pleasure' (v. 6), have become 'gossips and busybodies, *saying things they ought not to'* (v. 13), and by so doing are bringing the gospel into disrepute (v. 14)" (Gordon Fee, *1 and 2 Timothy, Titus,* New International Biblical Commentary 13 [Peabody, Mass.: Hendrickson, 1988], p. 70).

Question 5. Those who are educated (men, in Paul's culture) and are mature Christians would be more likely to see through the false teachers.

Study 7. Unity in Worship. 1 Timothy 2:1-15.
Purpose: To explore the implications of Paul's instructions in this passage for our churches.
Question 1. Verses 1-2, 5, 7, 8, and 9-10 suggest that Paul is seeking unity among the believers. He wants them to be rid of divisive anger, disputes (v. 8), and showing off (vv. 9-10). Additionally, as we saw in Study 6 (2 Timothy 3:1-9), the false teachers are creating controversy. Thus, Paul gives specific instructions to men and to women to deal with the results of the false teaching.
Question 2. Some might suggest that it is because it was men who prayed in public. However, 1 Corinthians 11:5 makes it clear that women both prayed and prophesied publicly. A more likely answer is that the men were having some type of dispute—perhaps over public prayer.
Question 3. These instructions probably relate to women being "swayed by all kinds of evil desires" (2 Timothy 3:6). "There is a large body of evidence, both Hellenistic and Jewish, which equated 'dressing up' on the part of *women* with both sexual wantonness and wifely insubordination" (Gordon Fee, *1 and 2 Timothy*, p. 71).
Question 4. Fee points out that in verse 11 Paul does say that "a woman should learn." Fee also suggests that *in quietness* (v. 11) is best translated as *in a quiet demeanor.* Fee thinks this is to prevent the woman from "talking foolishness" or being a "busybody" (see 1 Timothy 5:13; Gordon Fee, *1 and 2 Timothy*, p. 72).

The beginning of verse 12, "I do not permit," suggests that these are instructions for a specific situation. False teaching was a particular problem in Ephesus, as we have seen. "He is here prohibiting women *to teach* in the (house-)church(es) of Ephesus, although in other churches they prophesy (1 Cor. 11:5) and probably give a teaching from time to time (1 Cor. 14:26), and in Titus 2:3-4 the older women are expected to be good teachers of the younger ones" (Gordon Fee, *1 and 2 Timothy*, p. 73).

Women are also forbidden to "have authority over a man" (v. 12). "The word translated *authority*, which occurs only here in the NT, has the connotation 'to domineer.' In context it probably reflects again on the role the women were playing in advancing the errors—or speculations—of the false teachers and therefore is to be understood very closely with the prohibition against teaching. Rather, Paul concludes, *she must be* not *silent,* but 'in a quiet demeanor,' which exactly repeats the prepositional phrase of verse 11" (Gordon Fee, *1 and 2 Timothy,* p. 73).

Question 6. Verse 15 is very confusing and troublesome. One way this has been interpreted is that women "will be kept safe through childbirth" (NIV margin note). However, Fee points out that "Paul's use of the word *saved* throughout these letters disallows it (he always means redemption, from sin and for eternal life, as in 1:15-16 and 2:4)."

Another alternative would be to understand "childbearing" as referring to "*the* Childbirth, that is, through Mary's giving birth to Jesus, thus reversing the role of Eve by referring to the so-called *protevangelium* of Genesis 3:15. But besides this being a most obscure way of trying to say that, Paul nowhere else suggests that salvation is by the Incarnation or by Mary's deed."

Thus, Fee prefers the following reading:

More likely what Paul intends is that woman's salvation, from the transgression brought about by similar deception and ultimately for eternal life, is to be found in her being a model, godly woman known for her good words (v. 10; cf. 5:11). And her good deeds, according to 5:11 and 14, include marriage, bearing children (the verb form of this noun), and keeping a good home. The reason for his saying that she *will be saved* is that it follows directly out of his having said, "the woman came to be in transgression." (*1 and 2 Timothy,* p. 75)

Study 8. Interdependence. 1 Corinthians 11:3-16.

Purpose: To consider how men and women can complement one another and the role of authority in male-female relationships.

Question 1. For those who read 1 Corinthians from a traditional perspective, verse 3 demonstrates the principle of headship, "a common metaphor for authority." "It is the only symbolism that fits (certainly not source, for God is not the source of Christ). The Christian man's head is Christ, and the Christian woman's (not wife's) head is man, as also Christ's head is God (v. 3)" (Robert D. Culver, "A Traditional View," in *Women in Ministry*, p. 30). On the other hand, Alvera Mickelsen, who is supportive of women in ministry, says of this verse:

1 Corinthians 11:3 has often been read as a "chain of command." Yet all evidence indicates that "authority," "leader," "chief" were *not* common Greek meanings of head at the time Paul wrote this letter. The Greek meaning of *head* that fits best with the *context* here is "source" or "origin." Verses 8-12 are centered on origins. ("An Egalitarian View," in *Women in Ministry*, p. 196)

Question 4. "For a woman, taking off her head covering in public and exposing her hair was a sign of loose morals and sexual promiscuity. Paul says she might as well have her hair cut or shaved off. The shaved head indicated that the woman either had been publicly disgraced because of some shameful act or was openly flaunting her independence and her refusal to be in submission to her husband" (*The NIV Study Bible*, p. 1748).

Some find a lasting principle here which teaches that wives should show respect to their husbands by submitting to their authority. Others see this as instruction which was for the Corinthian church at that time in particular.

Verse 10 may raise some questions. *The NIV Study Bible* suggests that angels are "mentioned here because they are interested in all aspects of the Christian's salvation and are sensitive to decorum in worship" (p. 1748).

Question 6. These verses clearly teach that the sexes are interdependent.

Study 9. Requirements for Leaders. 1 Timothy 3:1-13.

Purpose: To look at the requirements for leadership in the church.

Question 2. Gordon Fee points out that the phrase *with proper respect* (v. 4) "probably means that they will be known for both their obedience and their generally good behavior." "There is a fine line between demanding obedience and gaining it. The church leader, who must indeed exhort people to obedience, does not thereby 'rule' God's family.

He *takes care of it* in such a way that its 'children' will be known for their obedience and good behavior" (*1 and 2 Timothy*, pp. 82-83).

Question 4. On the positive side they are to be "worthy of respect" (v. 8), having personal dignity. They are to "keep hold of the deep truths of the faith with a clear conscience" (v. 9). Literally, *deep truths* means "mystery" (Gordon Fee, *1 and 2 Timothy*, p. 87).

Question 6. There has been some debate over whether verse 11 refers to *wives* or *deaconesses*, as the Greek word *gynē* can mean either *wife* or *woman*.

In favor of *wives* is that the deacons are addressed on either side of this verse. It is also argued that one might have expected more detail if a third category were envisioned. In favor of *deaconesses* is the structure of the sentence itself, which is the exact equivalent of verse 8, both of which in turn are dependent on the verb *must* in verse 2 (thus implying three categories). It is further argued that had the wives of deacons been in view, Paul might have been expected to say *their wives* (as the NIV does without any warrant whatsoever). Since there was no word in Greek for "deaconess" . . . it is likely that *women* here would have been understood to mean women who served the church in some capacity. (Gordon Fee, *1 and 2 Timothy*, p. 88)

Study 10. The "Proper" Role. Luke 10:38-42.

Purpose: To explore the different kinds of roles which are available to us.

Question 4. Martha seems to think she's clearly in the right. Martha expects that Mary's proper place is working alongside her.

Question 6. Jesus is saying that learning from him is of primary importance.

Question 7. Find out how people in the group see women's roles. Do they think that Martha is setting an example for women—that they should do only certain kinds of things? Or do they see Mary as a model of a woman open to a variety of roles?

Question 8. Often we look down on Martha when we read this story, but the Marthas of the world are needed. Both kinds of functions are important, and both are godly.

Study 11. Ministering Together. Acts 18:18-28.
Purpose: To look at how husbands and wives can minister effectively together.
Question 2. Two possibilities are that Priscilla had a higher social status and/or that Priscilla took the lead in their ministry. In six New Testament references to this couple, three mention Aquila first and three mention Priscilla first.
Question 4. According to verse 24, Apollos was familiar with the Old Testament Scriptures. Verse 25 tells us that he had heard the preaching of John the Baptist. Thus, he knew of the prophecies about Jesus, but nothing of his actual life, death and resurrection on earth.
Question 5. Depending on the makeup of your group and their preferences, you might want to act out a short dialogue among the the three to re-create the conversation.

Study 12. Many Workers. Romans 16:1-16.
Purpose: To decide what kind of ministry we are called to.
Question 1. The women listed are Phoebe (v. 1), Priscilla (v. 3), Mary (v. 6), Junias (v. 7), Tryphena and Tryphosa (v. 12), Persis (v. 12), the mother of Rufus (v. 13) Julia (v. 15) and Nereus's sister (v. 15).
Question 4. We learn several things: Paul considers them partners. They risked their lives for him. All the churches know and respect them. A church meets in their home.